Pieces of Me

A Combat Veteran's Life

CM Daulton

TRIGGERPIECES

A TRAITMARKER BOOKS IMPRINT

Pieces of Me

A Combat Veteran's Life

CM Daulton

TRIGGER WARNING
This book contains potentially traumatic subject matter.

ATTRIBUTIONS
Interior Text Font: Apple Garamond
Interior Title Fonts: Apple Garamond
Editor & Cover Design: Robbie Grayson

ISBN: 978-1-64204-472-0

BOOK PUBLISHING INFORMATION
Published by Traitmarker Books
traitmarkerbooks.com
traitmarker@gmail.com

Printed in the United States of America

TABLE OF CONTENTS

Dedicated to my guardian angel:
You believed in me when I didn't believe in myself.
At one point, you loved me more than I did myself.
You gave me the key that unlocked so many doors
when I was lost and couldn't find my way.
Thank you from my heart to yours.

CM DAULTON
Specialist | Combat Veteran OIF 1 | Combat Injured
UNITED STATES ARMY

ACCLAIM FOR *PIECES OF ME*

★ ★ ★ ★ ★

Charlotte's poetry is moving, it is also tells a story of her as a person, a combat vet, a sister, a daughter, a aunt, and friend. It is pieces of her life she wants to share. It takes a lot of courage for her to have her poetry published. She is a very bright intelligent and loving person.

SUSAN FROGGE

Her poetry is inspiring to everyone who reads it touches you emotionally in your heart . She writes what she feels at that point of time and she puts all her feelings into her poems.

MARY HAMM

I have read some work that she has done and overall it was excellent. Each poem has a different meaning that one can relate too. Great job.

KAITLYN PRICE

Very passionate, strong intense feelings, telling how you felt..and feel. It tells of the depth from which you have come, to beauty that shows now...

VIVIAN BLUM

YOU'RE in my every thought
Inside every smile I hold you close
I look back on the memories we share
My grin becoming enlarged.

We've survived what should've destroyed us
Together we've been unstoppable
When we couldn't count on anyone else
We had each other.

The world could be shattering around us
I had you as my best friend and mother
With that in mind it made me Wonder Woman
I could conquer anything that stood in my way.

You motivated me to be a better woman
Your strength gave me the strongest hopes
Now you're not as strong & I'm lost, all alone
I have my biggest battle yet in front of me.

I know I'm not getting you back
I'm trying my best to prepare for what's next
How do I hang on? How do I keep strong?
How do I breathe without you once you're gone?

I'll cherish every second you said you were my girl
Every dance we shared at prom each year
Every selfie we ever took
Every story we shared... together!

Dedicated to my Mom.
My beautiful. My girl.

I feel you begin to slip away
You're not coming back to me
Lost inside your own mind
Trapped.

I've cried and laughed with you
Held your hand and kissed your cheek
I've told you how much you mean to me
All the while you've forgotten who I am.

This world has been cruel to your heart
One thing after another, you've held on
Time after time you've been let down
I seem to let you down the most.

All I ever wanted was for you to love me
I wanted to always feel worthy of this
To take care of your every need
Walk with you every mile so you're never alone.

The day will come soon when you're no longer here
The roses' scent and color fading
You'll be home at last in heaven
I'll be lost inside the memories left here on earth.

Dedicated to Mom

THE leaves just blew off your grave
Quickly blew my tears away
In the blink of an eye you were taken
Far quicker than the wind that blew.

Gone yet not forgotten, memories made
Pictures, books, treasured keepsakes
The love exchanged, love formed
Can be taken away in the blink of an eye.

Time has a lot of roles to play
A best friend, the enemy is shades of gray
Time travels, yesterdays are gone
Make your choices, make your plan.

Live without regrets, be so kind, so real
Always speak of how you feel
For you'll never get the chance again
To speak your truth and shine.

SHE taught me how to feel
The essence of red
A color I've always despised
I'm seeing it in a different light.

He taught me to always win the fight
It's better to persevere
Get up, quicker than you were knocked down
Never let your brother steal the victory crown.

Momma always talked perfection
Always wear a smile on the outside
Iron out those wrinkles, always be strong
Never wear your frown for long.

My lover showed me red
Daddy taught me to fight
Momma patched it up when I'd bleed
I learned many lessons in life.

WALK alongside of me
Not in front or behind
For as we walk this journey together
There are secrets we will find.

There's a whole new way to see life
No words needed
Holding hands, don't let mine go
I'll lead you to where you can be free.

We're smiling, giggling all the way
Just like we can only do
It's time, let the ocean waves crash over us
Cleansing our souls as I look upon you.

Somewhere in the sky above
Mysteries fall upon us
The sun shining, warming our hearts
I don't want our time to be rushed.

I took you to my safe place
Needed you to be there
Seagulls sing, seashells by our feet
Our toes roam the sand, as we stand bare.

A soldier says a prayer
On their way to a foreign land
Lord, place my family in your hands
For I know not if I'll see them again.

For battles I will fight, some I'll never win
Keep me safe so those I left behind will see me again
I know not if the enemy will shoot me
Not knowing if I'll live or if my brothers will die.

Each letter I get, I tuck it away
It's warming to my soul
It's not the same as being in my home
Lord, I pray, let me survive one more day.

I don't have time to wipe the blood or sweat
Gotta close my eyes in the day, guard the night
Sleep tight, America, on my watch you can
Watching my post, defending your rights.

Lord, if it's my soul you're gonna take
I will lay my life down at peace
I'm a strong warrior trained to survive
I'll go instead before those I fought beside.

MY brother, sleep tight
Rest in peace
Yes, sleep, I will shine your light
You can count on me.

You died in my mind
Never inside of my heart
I'll keep you in memory so others may find
Though you're in heaven, you're never far.

You made the ultimate sacrifice
The tears stream down my face
I wasn't there by your side
When you left soiled land for a better place.

Each year we gather in your memory
August 23 we lift your name in honor
We gather your family and battlebuddies
And call upon the father.

You may be gone though in spirit you're near
Roll call, you no longer answered
I miss hearing your voice so loud and clear
Longing to hold you but you're no longer here.

Dedicated to Sgt K Harris Jr
Operation Iraqi Freedom

I'M captivated by her beauty
Only her eyes draw me in
I can bare my vulnerability
She doesn't run.

When she smiles
She lights up the sky
As her lips tell me everything I know
How'd I become so fortunate?

I'm lifted up by her spontaneous will
I pull her close, I hold her tight
I feel, I just feel
I'm content with that.

All of her I breathe in
She makes me high
Without a drink
Without effort.

I'll speak with her in the room
Tradition doesn't break
I know my day will be smooth
Is she looking at the same moon?

1997 rushing off the cattle cars by our drill Sgt.
We found a square to shake down
Screaming in our ear's, *HURRY UP*
We discovered Ft Leonard Wood, MS.

Barracks, duffel bags up and down
Assigned battlebuddies, bunk, wall locker
Chow time, stand in line, ID cards to chin
Then we met, my best friend.

Each Sunday we went to church
Those who didn't, they have cleaning day
Weeks passed we eventually graduated
We never would be leaving Ft Leonard Wood, MS.

The time came when we left KY & Ohio
Letters written, phone calls made
Always kept in touch, tighter than blood
17 years, the best years of our lives.

Time can turn the colors of the leaves
        changing direction like the wind
It's ok, I understand, I patiently wait
I'm still here
 No matter how long as it takes.

I'm standing, never stopped, never will
We fought the same war, a little different
The war within turned the tables
Battlebuddies til the end of our journey.

I'm letting you know where I stand
Time won't always give us borrowed space
One life we have to live, my lost best friend
Please come around sometime before life's end.

Dedicated to PS

CANDLELIGHT

INSIDE a calming environment
Lights turned off
I stand in the shadow
With the feeling of release
Naked, bare
From head to toe
Tension escaping
I feel free
The woman in me
Cleansed by water
Washed with purity
Eyes closed
For moments I am inside a piece of heaven
Peace comforts me
Bubbles keep me afloat
No longer in darkness
Surrounded by candlelight.

My Child Within

I bend down to shake her hand
It's like we are meeting for the first time
Tears roll down my face, I look into her eyes
I've seen what she's been through
As I look inside of me.
Still I cry, I cry, I am squalling
As she puts my hand within hers
We walk together into this tunnel
The strength inside this little girl
Makes the weakness in me appear
I see once again I will become strong
I will stand one day with my head held high
Looking back on those moments of truth
Looking at my child within
Seeing her smile once again.

INNOCENCE GONE

INNOCENCE gone
I must continue to run
Trying hard to hide
All that's left is my will to survive.

I became an adult at six years of age
Still substituting the laughter for the tears
My soul cries & my lips catch the taste
Who knew that my innocence was taken
From the boy my parents raised?

Ignored femininity equals *unsafe*
I can't seem to escape this disturbance
Of losing myself to yet another rape
Is it me, am I the reason for another recurrence?
Innocence has left me, abandoned my right to a normal life.

All grown, buried the past beneath
Went to fight the war in Iraq
Just when I had to start to trust men
It happened once again.

I won't let the offenders take it easy
For this is something worth fighting for
I deserve to reclaim my innocence taken

I deserve so much more.
I deserve now what I offer to me alone
No more innocence to take:
INNOCENCE GONE.

ARMY OF ONE

A soldier works around the clock
A soldier knows not when to stop
A soldier does the job when others say it can't be done
In a soldier's army of one.

A soldier steps up when their name is called
A soldier picks you up when you're gonna fall
A soldier's goal is to get the battle won
In a soldier's army of one.

When a soldier closes their eyes they're really not asleep
They aren't at rest for they know no peace
A soldier must always be alert for the long haul
In a soldier's army of one.

This soldier will fight for your peace back home
This soldier won't let you down even when the hours get long
This soldier will defend all you wish to keep safe
This soldier's heart will warm your morning sun
In her Army of one.

EMPTY WORDS

EMPTY words, broken promises
You are still with me though
I spend my time reminiscing
Holding onto the thought of letting go.

You've always said we'd spend a lifetime together
Now you don't even call
I stand here patiently waiting on your forever
After you've already made me fall.

What am I supposed to hold?
When I'm not holding the other half of me
My arms are empty, I stand alone
Knowing your touch is all I need.

With this said, now I'll let you find your way
It takes so much inside to let us drift apart
If our love is nothing but a memory made
I will cherish this memory inside my heart.

I remember where she put those flip-flops
They never made it to the sand
All different colored ones piled up behind the door
The ones she'll keep hidden in the closet on the floor.

I remember the times she screamed my name
Her voice so serious
The look in her eyes was so fixated on what I had done
I just knew she was the one.

I remember when we counted change out of that coffee candlelight
It was so full and heavy
A quarter here, a dime there, all the coins in our hands
Nobody could top all the funny moments we had.

I remember last Valentines Day, running all over the place
Taking turns wrapping one another's things
Here is your chocolate, a bear, now go in there to roam
She stood in awe when she saw the candles, she read my poem.

I remember the way it all vanished in the air
The conversations turned to *I'm sorry* or *Really?*
Love washed down the drain, it went somewhere else
It lasted four months & now I have the greatest memories on
          my shelf.

I talk to her still and see that love still remains
She's in my phone, in thought
I remain in her heart as close as I can be
She'll always stand by my side, a best friend to me.

CONFUSED, lost, emotional, distraught
Who would've thought
Things led from one to another
A life is taken away like no other.

I ponder in my mind frequently
Is this ever meant for us to be?
You say *Hello* then *Goodbye*
In a blink of an eye.

I wonder with you up there
Is it possible for you to see me down here?
Are there rules in heaven I don't know about?
I can't comprehend, I can't figure things out.

I hear two versions of a home
One you live in on earth, one where you must live beyond
Please come back to me if only a short while
Let me talk with you, hold you one more time.

I think I've said I love you a thousand times before you passed on
Was it enough that I think I proved it, long after you've been gone
I loved you more, I proved it, now I'm trembling with my words
Should've, could've, would'ves makes my vision blurred.

THERE she is before me
Shining like a star
Nervous, palms sweaty
The first word that came to mind
Breathtaking
Her breath of fresh air
Adds perfume to my shirt
It never fades
Side by side sparks flew
Memories we continue to make
Our hearts still at peace
Wants, needs, purpose expressed
Skin on skin
Inside of me I feel renewed
No complications, a bond forever formed
I've searched countless years for that one touch mixed in affection
Never found such a willing soul
Each time I hold her inside my arms
I am content with our openness
She reached inside of me
I revealed myself bare
She's still here
That's uncommon for someone to be
Day to day we appreciate one another
We love each other's depth inside our individual souls
Simplicity never seemed so sweet
I love her in a different way
Her company validates who I am
I validate her being, her existence captivates my brown eyes
My grin from ear to ear, my smile never leaves
All because we have an unspoken truth
I have found my sunshine.

IF you could just love me
No words necessary to speak
If you could just have wanted me
Instead of passing me around
If you would've taken turns with Dad
Lying with me until I fell asleep
The monsters would've stopped coming after me
If you could've just paid a bit more attention
I would've felt you cared
If you would've just given me the time of day
I wouldn't have to guess how you feel
If you could've given me only affection
Maybe I wouldn't feel so alone.

If you would've stood up for me & watched over me
I could've taken a break from protecting you to feel safe
If you would've played with me
Maybe you'd know the things that make me laugh
If you could've taken responsibility as my mom instead of my sister
Maybe she would've learned the difference too
If you could've given me the talk about sex & puberty
Maybe I wouldn't look at it as though it's dirty
If you could've told Dad you loved him first
Maybe he would've known not every part of love hurts.

If you could've told me & reassured me I was good enough
Maybe I wouldn't have to seek your approval
If you would've changed my diapers
Maybe you could've seen I was being molested
If you would've loved me like you did hundreds of kids
Maybe I wouldn't question why I'm so hard to love
If you would've taught me how to communicate
Maybe I wouldn't keep everything bottled up inside

If you weren't so consistent with your guilt trips & manipulation
I wouldn't have to wonder what I'm doing wrong
If you wanted me around you more
You shouldn't have taught me to push someone away
If you would've helped teach me to drive & navigate
Maybe I wouldn't be so lost.

HER eyes tell me a story of a warm & perfect heart
Her voice is soothing to the soul as I hear her speak
She caught my attention when she reached out to me
I've never been the same since.

Time has no arms inside a clock, it passes effortlessly
When she cares she gives it all she's got
An abundance of love mixed with that comforting smile
Who could ask for anything else from such a woman as this?

One best believe she's worth fighting for all around the year
Don't break her heart, she's had enough of that
Her spirit is unbreakable, you can't put out her fire
If you're not ready for her to fall, promise nothing.

Once in a lifetime this kind of woman comes along
She's fierce, a woman with a seductive face
More importantly, it's all about the beauty that lies beneath
It's in the way she can hold you without holding you in her arms.

BETWEEN the sheets
I make love to you
I get lost inside your kiss
Your hands embrace my body
We dance around
Two hearts one soul
You spoke to me
With that come-here-now
Kind of voice
That gets me every time
I leave you breathless
As our bodies begin to ride.

I'M lost in the world of us
I'm intoxicated by your beauty
Captivated by your soul
 I never want to escape.

I've always heard but never did comprehend
What "love at first sight" was bound to have meant
It happened as it caught me unaware
She was just standing there.

If this is love, then what was before?
A whole new world, a side of love I never explored
Who am I as I look into her eyes?
Am I the one she's waited for all this time?

I've now seen what it means to have and to hold
A thought of us I'll never let go
I take her by the hand and her hand in mine
For our love is the dance of life.

I'VE fought in the trenches on the front lines
Took deadly risks sacrificing my life
With no time to think of anything else
I did all I could, I did my best.

I don't regret that my name was called
I am fighting for my country, giving my all
Back home others can go to sleep while I'm on watch
Living freely, going here, going there because they're safe while I'm
       on guard.

I know momma and dad worry, husbands and wives too
I'll be alright because they trained me on what to do
I'm prepared to make the ultimate sacrifice
Either way it turns out, I've done it so others live, my brothers
       won't die

If once I do make it home, I will remain a soldier
I may not return to whom I was before
Secrets, situations I may keep to myself
I am honored to be back to welcome all the hugs and smiles
And I will still do what it takes to save a life.

YOU agreed to take my name
When I placed that ring upon your hand
I never smiled so big when the moment came
You said *YES* and we started making plans.

You've enriched my heart, blessed my smile
Intoxicated me by your commitment and love
I look at you and I see our long future worthwhile
I see the beauty of us growing old & that's what I've dreamed of.

I promise to love you for better or worse, in sickness & health
I promise to lift you up if you need a soft place to fall
I promise that our life will be full of love's wealth
I promise the family will be even more strong.

I know when we say our vows aloud
We'll honor our love, our lives together
I believe completely in what we've found
I believe in our forever!

You've agreed to take my name
You've enriched my heart, blessed my smile
I promise to love you & be your soft place to fall. We'll honor our
commitment enriching our lives as one.

I scratch the surface, I only feel the sand
I clench my fist, I grit my teeth
Angry, defeated, I don't understand
Why you had to leave.

I can't live through another nightmare
My thoughts vs the pain
I left war to return home to the ones who care
I came home why do I feel the shame?

They buried you back home
No goodbyes from here we said
We saluted, we cried, held our own
As your dog tags were laid to rest.

A part of me inside died with you
I can't bring you back if I could
It's not over, it can't be over, it can't be true
If I ask you to come back, I know you never would.

Each year I'll continue to meet you at your grave
With our battlebuddies as we do each year
Paying tribute to our fallen brother, for us you saved
The leader of the pack who knows no regrets or fear.

Dedicated to my fallen battlebuddy Sgt Harris

I'M holding onto the thought of you
For I no longer hold you in my arms
You slipped right through my fingers
You couldn't love me anymore... why?

I put a ring on your hand, you said *Yes*

I gave you my all, I gave you nothing less
I sacrificed, I gave you patience & understanding
I'm lost and broken
You care no more about my feelings.

I learned that you couldn't tell me *I love you*
I yearned to hear *I miss you from miles away*
I longed to hear that you couldn't imagine a day without me
I've cried, I've wondered why you refused to make me feel loved.

I love you still, I know I can't be who you love or need
I harbor no hard feelings, I just want you to be happy
With or without me, I'm gonna live like I had before you
I will smile when I hear your name, I'll only hold you in thought.

I watch the tears come out of your eyes
I read the comments of grief you express
You're lost and feeling alone
What can I do to unbreak your heart?

I search the scriptures to find you relief
Just realized that's not the only thing you need
It's just gonna take time to heal your spirit
I'll be right there to help you through it.

Just take your memories and hold on
Remember the good times with him and smile
For he wouldn't want you to give up on life
He wouldn't want you to cry.

He and the angels are watching over you
You can't feel his touch but he's there
It's your loss heaven's gain
Remember they all love you the same.

I wash my hands of your thoughtless ways
I'm rid of all your lies and deceit
I walked away and you never asked me to stay
I don't want your empty explanations, just leave.

I choose to erase the mistakes I made
Though the words can't be erased
Nothing is wrong when feelings fade
I choose to rise above the unexpected pain.

I'll let you sit on the pedestal you created
I never once put you up there
Be careful before you fall down with devastation
For I'll no longer open myself up to care.

Never let my name fall on your lips
We've now reached the end of the road
Never expected things to turn out this
No regrets, lesson learned, now I must go.

I wanna escape into places I've never been
Seduced with thoughts of you
Drive down the road less traveled
Tank full.

Swing by and pick you up unannounced
To see your smile would be intoxicating
Taking you on this ride
Overdue.

The ocean calms my soul
Waves crashing over our feet... splash
I lift you off the ground & spin you 'round
Refreshing.

I wanna escape into places I've never been
Swing by and pick you up unannounced
Waves crashing over our feet
Seduced with thoughts of you.

VULNERABLE

Heart wide open
Scared, anxious
No bounds
Hands tied
Mouth dry
Chained
Repeated song
No pen to paper
Lying in wait
No clock
Just time.

SHE used to keep up with daddy's keys
Every time he'd forget where they are
She is now lost in her memories
As she wanders around the halls.

She'll start out shuffling her feet
To the nurse's desk she'll roam
She tries to remember the last time she saw me
How she wishes she was home.

She tries to fight her sleep
She carries much weight on her shoulder
She tries to put the puzzle back together with her memory
As I sit with her and hold her.

I miss you, mom, I'm never leaving my girl
I wish you didn't feel so alone
My tears fall like rain, you are my world
My arms will always be your home.

Dedicated to my mom..
She has Alzheimer's.

I bleed much faster
The more you bruise my soul
Piercing me with the dagger of your words
Spilling from your tongue.

You've hurt me so much
The rust is decaying your efforts
To bring me down
I still rise above.

You've turned more colder
I no longer seek to meet you halfway
Keep denying everything
You love it when the truth slaps you in the face.

YOU came into this world so tiny and strong
You changed my life without knowing
I brought you home from the hospital
From that moment on we were inseparable.

Your laughter is still heavenly as when I first heard it
I grin from ear to ear each time I hear the sound
You sure grew up fast, I memorized every milestone
Now, my once little girl, is walking down the aisle.

All throughout my life, you stole my heart
You made life worth living even more
When this world beat me up or dragged me down
One look at you was all it took for me to grin once more.

As you stand before all who loves you
Taking your vows before God
I'll stand there in amazement of my little girl
The most beautiful bride ever seen in the world.

Dedicated to my princess, my niece:
Anna Marlene 10/5/17

YOU lay beside me asleep
Your hand on my heart... I'm at peace
It's been two years since you were in my arms
I can't breathe.

You called me out of the blue
I came running to you in the rain
Fate brought us back to how it used to be
We did the rest.

My fingers played in your hair
You had me sing you to sleep
My hand in yours, fingers entangled
My hand is your hand.

No, I don't mind, I'm not jumping to conclusions
Just to the picture-perfect memories
I feel alive and myself again
These are just my thoughts of us.

WHEN you came into my life
I hadn't known about love before
I went through the motions of relationships
Never imagined that I could love until you.

You came along at the perfect time
At first, in my dreams, then in front of me
Like a knight in shining armor
You swept me off my feet.

I'm living in my own fairytale like Cinderella
I am ready, willing and able to complete you
As you will wake up to only me
Coming home to our family every single day.

As we place these rings on our fingers
This circle represents our neverending love
I will hold you until my dying day
I will love you to beyond infinity.

I will take you, cherish you, love you
I promise to honor us each morning as I wake
Each night I will remind you how you bring me hope
Of better things yet to come.

Written for the wedding of Anna & Ryan.
Dedicated to them.

COUNTRY concert in Vegas
The crowd singing every song
Cheering, clapping, cowboy hats in the air
Good times, Beer, Cheers!

Crazy old man, a dozen shot guns stored in his hotel room
Bullets grazing people's skin
Killing 59 Americans, wounding 500 more
Loved ones shield their loved ones
A stranger dies in another's arms.

No, this didn't happen on foreign soil
It happened right here in Vegas
The city that parties til the next morning
The city that gambles money now gambling with people's lives.

Swat teams, police, sirens, chaos
Who's alive and wounded? Who's dead?
Families worried sick, will they see their loved ones again?
The ones who are saved were pushed from harm's way.

America in mourning, flags at half-staff
News media updating every chance they can
Just a country-feel-good concert
Crazy old man took freedom to breathe... away.

Dedicated to a tragedy

IT'S your favorite time of year again
I can never make up my mind about it
I feel you more, surrounded by warmth
I hate it even more because Fall took you away.

Looking at this picture
I can hear you tell me you want a copy
Only to scotch tape it to your in the study
I miss seeing your favorite pictures on that wall.

I miss the times you called out my name without fail
I miss hearing *Hey Char... I love you*
Hey Char, turn it on Gunsmoke for daddy
Hey Char, look at those beautiful, colored leaves.

You always said everything on your heart
Never holding anything back
Now that you've been gone all this time
I hear you saying *Hey Char... daddy's right here.*

I'll go on missing you, Dad
Yeah, mom is doing alright too
Laura, the girls and I are missing you
And your great grandbabies are growing up fast.

Dedicated to Dad:
It's been 9 long years since you passed.

FORTY-two years ago, a girl was born
Chubby legs, the widest smile
I only wanted mom without fail
Everyone took turns babysitting me.

Five-years old, kindergarten bound
Long, brown, the most curly hair
Cheerleading mascot, going to all of the games
I loved to play possum.

Mom and dad took turns staying until I fell asleep
No want for bedtime stories, I wanted to hear them sing
Jesus loves me, this I know, you are my sunshine
Monsters under my bed, my dad lay with me until I fell asleep.

Brother left home, then my sister soon followed
I was left behind, lonely teenager coming into her own
Mom & dad had a tight leash on their baby
I got sassy with mom one too many times
I was stubborn and I came by it honestly.

High school, I was on the basketball & softball teams
I was the unpopular one, I didn't have the finer things
Posters covered my walls
Parker had my heart.

Senior year, senior pictures taken
My first job at McDonald's, I started smoking cigarettes
Senior prom with a blind date, pictures taken
Driver's Ed, in loving memory, graduation day.

College-bound, brother still in the Air Force
My sister had tried college then marriage
Still I was left behind, Adulthood tough
Hellbent to make it on my own.

I found the piece of my own puzzle
I was free, I cried, I fought my feelings for a girl
I was taught it was wrong, I wrestled with that demon
Inside I distanced myself, hidden secret.

I enlisted in the Army, mom could've spit nails
Basic Training graduation, my dad's proudest moment
Met my forever friend and battlebuddy
Didn't know what to expect, new unit, Private.

My 7th year of serving, 9/11... later deployed
I was in love with Amy, I had to leave
I said goodbye, new unit, mom dropped me off
Who writes their will at 26?

Ft. Campbell, thoughts racing, who would have my back?
Airport hanger, I said my final farewell on the phone
God, I'm not in control, bring me back home
Harris made the ultimate sacrifice, I died too.

Army retired, disabled veteran, nightmares
Mom & Dad helped me fight the war at home
Who had I become? Nobody knew me anymore
My "Guardian angel" gave me the gift of life.

Time to tuck my parents in bed, health fading
Fix their meals, roles of parenting reversed
Mom diagnosed with a cruel disease, immobile
The angels carried Dad home, ½ of me gone.

Family divided, going your own way
Grandkids grown, great-grand kids born
New diagnosis, mom's health fading fast
Memory sometimes slips, nursing home bound.

Life has taught me how to survive and smile
I found happiness in me, loving myself
Who would've thought I'd still be standing?
I am here, I'm a survivor!

WE'VE been through so much
Side by side, ride or die
We've been there when nobody else was
Sometimes a friendship is no longer enough.

I take, I take, now I'm just fed up
I'm tired, so tired of your emotional abuse
I can no longer keep going on
I'm such a bad friend you accuse.

I know you feel entitled like you own me
Those actions aren't for sale
I've loved you & love you still, what will be will be
If you only realized how much I care.

I don't want to call it quits
My options have run out
I've grown weary, torn down from this
I'm not as strong anymore so I take my bow.

What could've been would be beautiful
· It had the potential of being more great
I'm tired of being nothing, who could be hopeful?
I'm already gone nothing left to say.

THERE'S more to me than my body
I'm not just a gentle soul
I claim me
I AM WOMAN... HEAR ME ROAR!

There's more to life than just experiences
If you want something run like hell to reach it
No matter what it takes reach out
Don't look down, arise and go forth.

I am meek, you can't tame me
There's a fire burning inside
Everyone's afraid to touch
Though they want to play with the flames.

Don't put your hand under my shirt
Don't tease me knowing I want to kiss your lips
Don't say one thing and want another
Unless you want all of me.

Capture the hidden part of me
There's an edge to me, a mystery
I'm afraid for anyone to see this side of me
Those who have, damaged me, it's unsafe.

Come to me, show me your effort
I don't want to push you away
It's all I know, push back
If you are wanting to come close.

Are we just one-sided?
Are you wanting to touch upon my heart?
I can't read your mind
Don't send me mixed signals.

Run away with me
We've fought this long enough
The candle only burns if you light it
Don't be afraid for I want you to explore all of me.

PS I claim me!!!

I'M losing control inside
It's hard to see you interested in another
Why can't you see me?
I'm right here yet you look past me.

You say you are wanting this and that
When you could have it all
Have you ever loved somebody so much
That every breath you take, she breathes you?

I'm more than anything she is to you
She doesn't know your passion
She's not your sunlight in the morning
She makes you want things she can't give.

I get lost in every word you say
I feel you when I lay down as I close my eyes
I would walk to the end of the world for you
I want to spend every second with you for the rest of your life.

Dedicated to JM

I'M waiting for you patiently
You're close enough to touch
Every night I listen to your playlist
Holding myself, aching to tell.

Every second you're in between
My slideshow of you repeats
Each time I watch it, my arms are around you
I imagine I'm in front of you face-to-face.

This has gone on for so long, excruciating
I'm running out of reasons to run and hide
Tell me I'm not alone in this fairytale
Tell me you're aching for my touch.

I have what it takes to bring you happiness
I could capture your stars & bring down the moon
Anything no matter what it takes
I know you want me too, you're hesitating.

I'm sitting in the middle of this room
Surrounded by candlelight, rose petals covering the floor
My feelings are bare, I'm vulnerable
Just make it to me.

These words used too often in this world
Now when said by others, meaning lost
I have to take the chance though I'll be turned away
Just keep your head down and make it to me.

Once you look into my eyes, see me smiling back at you
It's then you'll know you can love me
Nothing else matters, just you and I
Open your heart & you'll find me there.

WET

Surrounded by candlelight
A glass of wine
My thoughts in that certain space
I hold onto the night.

I ran into an old flame
To see her just wasn't the same
Time sure did show me how much I've grown
I'm much better now that we're done.

We are better as friends
It was better that we came to an end
There's no bitterness, no regrets
Just a part of my past I won't forget.

It's good to see she's happy for I am too
Things are less complicated now that we're through
We've both matured, reached new heights
It no longer matters who was wrong or right.

Time heals all wounds, no feelings left
The heart is aware when things are left unsaid
Memories come, feelings go, no shame
Things didn't work out, circumstances are to blame.

Now I'm leaving, closing the door
I've moved on, there's nothing more
No hard feelings, I'm glad we put the past behind
I wish you the best & all the love you can find.

I want to push you to the furthest place... I can't
I want to know what your hands feel like... I can't
I want to taste your lips like the wine... I can't
I want to be your love song... .I can't.

You don't see me, you look right through... you can't
You don't feel the way I do... you can't
You don't know how much you love me... you can't
You have no idea that I'm head-over-boots... you can't.

Others like you, you don't know you're missing out...
        ya'll can't
Others call studs like me sweet yet you want to be friends...
        ya'll can't
Others want studs like me yet settle for a bad boy...
        ya'll can't
Others will never love studs like me, your loss...
        ya'll can't.

If you and I are going to be, reciprocation a must... we can't
If I want to love you completely, you don't... we can't
If you love me, say it, give me a sign, I'll run to you. We can't
If we are feeling something together, let's show it..
WE CAN .

Do I fear these sleepless nights?
Am I unconsciously aware?
I'm conflicted, confined to these walls
While the world is sleeping peacefully.

If I close these eyes for a moment
I know where they'll take me
Back to the sand I tread once more
Back to the start of the same tour of duty.

Do I fear the sleepless nights?
Am I unconsciously aware?
I stand guard at the entrance
Wide awake for the enemy, wide awake for me.

If I close my eyes for the moment
I want racing thoughts no more
I'm tired of going back to this war
The heat in which makes my face feel cold.

I'll go back into battle tonight
I don't give up, there's a risk I'm willing to take
No soldier backs down from the challenge
Do I fear these sleepless nights? Fuck No!

SINCE I was a young teen, I dreamed of you
In my head I knew the color of your hair
I knew that smile way before I've seen it
I knew all about you when I knew nothing of love.

It's ok that I've never met you, we're not there
I've carried you beneath my shirt in the pocket of my heart
I knew I would never know where to look
For that's where fate took over.

I played with your long hair
Holding you inside my arms, your head on my chest
I've seen that we'll have all the time in the world
To love each other our whole life through.

Last night I saw us laughing uncontrollably
Then your eyes found mine yet again
You told me you loved me for so long
I whispered *I knew I loved you before we met.*

I no longer look at the clock for time
I only look at you, such beauty before me
The search is over, it's been over
I saw you long ago when you stole my heart.

I knew there'd come a day fate would introduce us
I've talked to you without speaking
I've made love only to the thought of you
I found my soulmate in all of these dreams.

PS I knew since I was a kid what the love of my life looks like

I am far from perfect yet I know my worth
I need no one, all I need is me
I won't let me down, I won't betray
I have all I need, I will survive.

People play dress-up, disguised as friends
I have I've-seen-it-with-my-own-eyes issues
Trust, like I love you, are words without meaning
Dressed up to look like beautiful words from the heart.

Fitting in comes with a price, nobody has your back
You lose your integrity, your credibility will crumble
Don't follow others, you'll lose your way
To the point of no return.

Being young and naive can't be an excuse
Everyone bears responsibility in a choice
I pledge my allegiance to God, country, family
I know the enemy, the enemy knows not me.

When the only choice you have is to rise
To become someone greater than yourself yesterday
To stand and fight with honor when it's you against the world
Is not to fear confrontation.

TODAY I hope to see a red bird or two
I hope it flies right in front of me
I'll burst out *Happy birthday, Dad!* to you
As you sit upon the branch of your favorite tree.

I'll thank God for letting me see you again
I'll praise him for making you my father
For the memories we made back then
Makes me more blessed to be your daughter.

I remember when I used to sit in your lap
The way you'd lie with me until I fell asleep
Those were the good times I wish I had back
Those times will always stay with me.

Now as I wave and watch you fly away
It's time you go back home
I'm just glad I saw you on that branch today
Instead of celebrating your birthday alone.

I'M conflicted with my thoughts
As you push then pull me back to you
There are things that can't be bought
Those things created with the power of two.

There's no ocean I wouldn't cross
There's no terrain I wouldn't hike
To reach you when you feel uncertain in your thoughts
I will take you by the hand each and every time.

When you're feeling weary and scared
I'll always be your soft place to fall
You can always count on me to be there
I'll be the reassurance you need to carry on.

When you're not sure about what you feel
I won't pressure, I won't demand anything
You know I am where you are, sit... still
You're the woman I've longed for in fairy tales & dreams.

It's rare when someone can make scars slowly fade
Who makes happiness out of tragedies?
Who can turn fear into beautiful mcmories made?
Who can teach you love without boundaries?

She's who you've searched for in all the wrong places
She makes believe in something you can't see
Love when found, you must embrace
Before it becomes a distant memory.

I want to make love to your thoughts
No need to touch just yet
I embrace your mind and the contents
I'm kissing you, my lips on yours.

I just want to look in your eyes and stare
I wasn't born until I looked into them
My hands have squeezed your hand
They become one hand.

I've told you a thousand times
How you sneak into all of my dreams
You have me mesmerized, speechless
I'm trembling, you give me butterflies.

You dance before me, bare, I'm moved
You let me stay, I play your Spanish lullaby
I make love to you as though this is my first time
Take me, I've been yours so long.

In my imagination, I've serenaded you
On a bed of roses, I pick you up, we lay
Candles lit, our bodies sway
I can make love to your thoughts as I make love to you.

LONG blonde hair falling on her shoulders
Her green eyes staring into my brown
Those lips they all add up when it comes to her
Always smiling, how I wish dreams had sound.

She works hard for something she loves
She's all in or nothing, I like that kind of girl
She challenges me, assures me I'm enough
Her voice carries me to a better world.

She's driven, achieving what she wants
She hangs onto the fears of losing someone again
I share them for love is greater than the hunt
It will come, it is going to last, be still my friend.

Her beauty radiates the surface, better than the moon
She is watchful, she can sense everything in motion
Patiently waiting, nothing will happen to soon
Seeking something between us, deeper than emotion.

I touch you with my thoughts
I'm holding you tight inside my arms
Touch
I'm making love to your soul.

I want to ignite this fire inside of you
Lay you down into ecstasy
Kiss every inch of you
Touch without touching you.

Put my fingers inside your hair
Teasing your body with my tongue
Tasting all of you
Until the sun comes up.

Turning your body upon your stomach
Your hair pulled back to me
Your moan, you beg me to take you
I know just what I want to do.

My fingers all over your body
Up and down, tracing you as you squirm
You never came out and asked
You just wanted me to take you into me.

The heat continuing to rise between our bodies
I taste you, I feel warm, all inside of you
I'm all in, you can track my movements
You have all of me melting into you.

Tell me you want me stop, you can't
You love it too much
Nobody has moved you like this
You can only deny it so long.

You can only cum when I tell you too
Your fingernails all into my back
You had me since you first noticed
I've had you since hello.

SHE radiates such beauty in a picture-perfect frame
I talk to her all the time, though I never say a word
Nervous, palms sweaty, this chance I'm gonna take
I'm going to talk to her.

Every picture she shares, every smile
Has won my heart over time and time again
I want to sit and talk with her awhile
Even though I'm just her friend.

I don't stand a chance if I speak about how I feel
Do I say it anyway? Vulnerability never safe
It's hard to explain something I've tried to reveal
It's been so long since I've felt this way.

If only I could just work up the nerve
I'd speak from deep inside my soul
If I wrote 1,000 letters to her
Maybe she'd see the truth unfold.

I realize this won't get me nothing more
I've got to get this off my chest
She's the waves crashing onto the shore
She's happiness.

THE music starts, I hold you in frame
Our feet they move in sync
I imagine us in the center of the floor
I'm taking the lead.

We touch, we hold each other in frame
I lift you off your feet, your hair falls off your shoulders
I've never been in heaven like this
We sway.

The music puts heat between us on the floor
Our eyes are locked in song
I'm nervous, heart pounding strong
I want only you to keep me on the floor.

Can you feel me melting into you?
Wondering if my steps are right
You look at me with assurance
Then I let you down towards the floor.

We take our bow with smiles on our face
I imagine you falling into me
Though this would only be perfect
If what I imagined was real.

YOU sing to me every time we talk
More clear than an orchestra of strings
I hear you play like that Spanish guitar
It's music defining the depth of how you reach me.

You're a breath of fresh air like a beautiful sky
Simple with an edge yet simple with a twist
You add your spice in that I've never tried
Just enough for me to taste a little bit.

Your authentic self is food for the soul
You enrich everything and give life sound
I want to dig much deeper than what I show
Understanding you, a book I can't put down.

I'm a beautiful disaster. A path that is rare
The ocean waves crashing onto the shore
The clouds that you can't rearrange with a stare
A mystery that you desire to explore.

Dedicated to JM

TOMB OF THE UNKNOWN

To those who didn't make it home
Laid to rest in the tomb of the unknown
Many found on different kinds of soil
They gave their blood just the same in different wars.

In a country where they guarded out of respect
Daily marching, changing of the guard protect
A grave where names weren't identified
Bled the same, fought and died.

Rain, snow, hail or sun
They will march many miles until their shift is done
The Commander-in-chief places a wreath in front
In memory of the fallen daughters and sons.

As long as blood runs through my veins
I'll render my salute every Memorial Day
Every day my heart will be your home
Rest easy, soldiers in the *Tomb of the Unknown.*

MY life changed when I became your daughter
When I became an adult you knew what advice to give
You knew the mistakes I would make ahead of time
Yet you let me make them so I could learn.

My life changed when I told you *Goodbye* when I left for war
I didn't know if I would get to see you again
So I begged God to bring me back home
In return I would tell the world of his love.

My life changed completely when you became disabled
I knew how hard it hurt you when you couldn't work anymore
It took away your joy and abilities yet you persevered
You are the strongest woman I know.

My life changed when you got that silver in your hair
I realized all I took for granted was fading
I realized the meaning of life as I've taken care of you
When your mind & body has played tricks on you.

I've seen mostly all the tears that fell
Times you were afraid, not knowing the outcome
Those times you wanted us kids home
The smiles filled with pride as you became Mamaw.

My life changed when I had to put you in the nursing home
I knew that it's not the place you wanted to go
I've held you in my arms when you felt you didn't know how much
        more your body could take
The many times I wanted your pain on me instead.

Now these golden years I'll cherish even more
I promise you won't ever be alone
I promise to help you remember in times you might forget
My life will change forever once you're gone.

LOVING WAY

LOVING WAY a street name
A street where my life changed
I saw it before me today
It took me back to yesterday.

The first time I felt pain
The first time my child within changed her name
The first time her lips kissed my doll
The first time Charlotte felt it all.

The first time he forced my hand
The first time little Charlotte couldn't understand
The first time it penetrated through my little soul
The first time I had no control.

At the home of 627 Loving Way
What was so *loving* about that day?
Avoidance, withdrawn I used to be
LOVING WAY isn't so loving to me.

LIGHTNING strikes within my soul
There's a fire in my eyes
I love that you make me feel like new
I hang onto every word.

Beautiful like the lyrics in a song
You're far from perfect this I know
Somehow you're the exclamation point
You highlight all of me.

Guitar strumming, lights down low
Candles lit as my voice begins to sing
I had it all figured out until I looked upon your face
A picture is worth a thousand words.

Let me see you bare not in the way you think
Let me see all of you through my eyes
You're gorgeous, you don't see yourself as I
What I see goes beyond skin-deep.

I have a slideshow of thoughts
A map of your existence leading me to you
There are no tickets for the show
For my thoughts of you are priceless.

Take me down a two-lane road
I want to get lost only to find my way
Take me there, where I've longed to go
Destination unknown.

Dedicated to JM

YOU don't know what you got til it's gone
That friend who backs your every word
The friend from afar
You know the one, the one you love to ignore.

One day it's going to be too late
You regret with the should've, could've, would've
Look in the clear mirror what you take for granted
Don't continue to throw everything away.

Distance becomes the choice I have to make
I realize my worth, I am enough
To someone else I'll be the sun
While you still play in the dark.

You let others decide who can fit in
Who is only around at their convenience
Over someone who would fight for your honor
And catch you when you're falling apart.

Don't blame anyone for your choices
Don't blame the one you threw away
You're going to wake up & miss me at some point
Seeing that I'm priceless to another.

I got the much-dreaded call
My friend called & told me you were gone
Tears fell like rain, my feelings raw
I didn't expect this at all.

She was shy until she got to know you
She kept to herself, quiet, life gave her pain
She kept going strong with all she had been through
She was no stranger to the rain.

There was more to love if you gave her your time
She was a loving soul, a giving friend
If you were in need she was the giving kind
Her spirit shined like a crystal from within.

She was a woman of truth and character
She accepted nothing less and nothing more
Humble, sweet, with a heart of gold about her
Her heart was an open door.

In memory of Roxanne Raynes

IF you can't handle me at 100-proof
If you can't handle me loving you
If you can't handle me worshiping you at your feet
If you can't handle me adoring you, I'll leave.

Right woman, wrong time
I've put everything on hold
Hoping I'd win your heart
On my own.

I know you like me but you will never love
You'll never notice me not worth your thoughts
I'll just keep my dream alive a little while longer
I'll let myself down gently so you won't have to.

I just want to know where you'll be
I'll settle for blending in the crowd
We don't have to speak, I'll just be content
Knowing we share the same space.

She won't ever answer when you call
You love her the way I love you
A million miles away, she can't handle you at 100-proof
I'll stay here in our shared space... content.

Love me too someday
Tell me to stay
I'm the right one, wrong time
Don't let me slip away.

YOU danced across my dreams again last night
You were wearing the smile I gave
You told me to tell you everything I love
All I said was *You!*

You ran into my arms willingly
As your eyes looked towards mine
My fingers brushed your hair back
Then we kissed.

I fell in love with you time and again
I hadn't worked up the nerves to tell
Don't you know by the way I sing your song?
I wrote this just for you.

I don't keep track of the time anymore
Since the day I gave you ownership of my heart
What reasons do I give for this?
You've had my heart since the beginning of time.

Candles lit all around the room
I lift you off the ground, arms around you tightly
You whisper *Baby, I've loved you too*
Our clothes fall to the floor... we make love.

YOU raised me to always stay the course
Never surrender you don't have a choice
Work hard until you can't work no more
Always remember love is worth fighting for.

When you feel sorrow, don't mourn for long
When you fail, bounce back more strong
When you smile, remember I'm smiling too
When you're angry, don't hold it inside of you.

When life gets complicated, keep the faith
Always complete the task whatever it takes
Things may not go your way at times
But my sweetheart, that's part of life.

There will come a day momma will be gone
I'm not going to forget you, I want you to go on
Dig deep inside your soul, you'll feel me near
No matter what happens, I'll be with you here.

Dedicated to Mom

SILVER dog tags dangling on a chain
Thousands and thousands of names
Engraved blood type, social security
Representing those who died to make us free.

Take a moment of silence and bow your head
For those who didn't return home, whose families wept
Don't take their sacrifice in vain
Take a knee in remembrance of Memorial Day.

Back then they dug through the trenches
Now they're fighting in the sand, no fences
These wars are fought for our country and flag
The debt paid-in-full, no questions asked.

Eat your barbecue, drink those cold beers
Tell me, will you remember why you're here?
While our brothers and sisters render their salute
For our country, our red, white and blue!

Dedicated to those who died

YOU say you want someone to love you
To sweep you off your feet
You don't want the one that can
You want the fantasy.

The way music takes you into the dance
You want love to take you to new heights
You don't notice it's staring you in the face
Out of mind, outta sight.

You say you've longed to be held, caressed
For someone to be your last call of the day
It's not enough that you're someone else's dream
You haven't really noticed yet.

I can't make you love me, so pass on by
Everything has been laid out on the table
You can't turn a song into the dance
With the perfect love you hope to find.

YOU'VE written neverending letters
Written all inside my heart
It's been so long since I have felt better
I have with you every second since we've talked.

You bring out the best of me, have I ever said?
Have I let you know how crazy I am about you?
You had me from hello, you're always in my head
I haven't let anyone completely in, it's long overdue.

I want you to wake up close inside my arms
Feeling my heartbeat, it's beating strong
You've taught me there's no place that far
When you've waited for the right one for so long.

I can't wait to pull you close, hold you tight
To watch you fall asleep, to see you fall for me
I could tell you everything, kiss you every night
I'll patiently wait for the day where you're right where you
        should be.

I see the setting sun, no more days I'll spend alone
The love we'll share will remain in every smile
Our laughter will echo the words in song
Your arms make me feel like home.

SHE doesn't know how beautiful she is
How she makes my heart skip a beat
Just how warm her eyes make me feel
Just how tight I hold her in my thoughts.

She doesn't know what I'd give to be her #1
To be the song she always loves to sing
To feel her hands entangled with mine
To have her lie her head inside my arm.

She doesn't know she's the perfect fit for me
All the times I could picture us together
All the times I wanted to say *She's all I ever hoped I'd find*
If she could look into my heart she'd see.

Today I'm gonna let her know what's inside
I'm going to wipe my sweaty palms and breathe
I'm going to tell her somehow I loved her right away
I'm going to let her see I"m worthy of her love.

I lay here in the darkness
Waiting to be next to your skin
I've felt the fire, it's still burning
It's keeping me warm.

I long to hold you in the dance
Your feet upon mine, are my feet
You're taking my breath away
You've taken all of me in this song.

How much longer will it take?
I've waited so long to touch your soul
I've waited all my existence.

Tell me when you close your eyes
I want to be the one your dreams
You'll feel that fire, it's burning
I'll be there patiently waiting in the heat.

WE met in college, our first date he proposed
I didn't know enough about this man to do such a thing
I looked at him like he was crazy when I said *No*
I didn't know I would end up wearing a diamond ring.

February 23, 1964, I walked down the aisle
You looked like all your dreams came to life
I wore a beautiful dress & you in the tux formed my smile
We were announced as husband and wife.

Our first child came in 1966, a girl in 1968, a girl in '75
They were stubborn, cute, funny & smart
They grew up too fast, time sure could fly
To this day, each one wins us over in our hearts.

It was 2008 when my husband passed away
I love him, he loved me, he always let me know
It's our anniversary, I still remain your bride
My heart will always will be yours because that's where it belongs.

Dedicated to my parents. I wrote this as she said these things to me:
that's why I wrote it as if she did.

INTERESTED, I don't know how you can't believe
I've been hurt too, let down & deceived
When it comes to matters of the heart
I always take them seriously.

Every time I see you through the phone
I've stopped living in darkness, no longer alone
When I hear your voice, stars can't shine so bright
You take things to another level, to a higher light.

I like watching your every single smile
Your expressions make my worries disappear for awhile
I like you just as you are, please never change
When the going gets tough don't just run away.

Sometimes we can't control one minute to the next
It's too early to throw away our potential yet
Disappointment, I know the feeling all too well
You can be assured of the way for you I care.

"Seeing through the phone" refers to "face time"

I saw your picture, I just stared again and again
Quickly my heart melted, I said I'd settle as friends
I must've sounded like a love-struck fool
I had to talk with you.

You told me how you had work to do
I told you I was working on me too
One thing led to another, fate intervened
You lit a fire inside of me.

Last night we saw each other for the first time
We opened our video chat online
You expected my voice to sound different
I never knew your smile was heaven-sent.

We laughed, questions asked, answers given
Tried to play a song about my kind of feelings
You put your hair behind your ear, that's all it took
Until you gave me that come-and-kiss-me look.

Morning rolls around, I rushed for my phone
I couldn't help but wonder if I was up alone
Did you hear me in your dreams last night?
Whispering *Now there's no end for us in sight.*

I can't rush, I can't lose with love anymore
I'm tired of trusting, hurting, rushing like before
I'm too broken but I know all I want is you & me
Let's fight, let's love not lose, love each other indefinitely.

I will pick you up on your front door step
Roses in hand, a date only for us, you'll never forget
You'll be dressed up, I'll be in the shirt & tie
I'll open the door to the best date of all time.

JESUS whispers *It's time to come home*
In a moment's notice she was gone
The machines were working overtime
She donated everything, all her organs inside.

When you bury your child, it's hard to comprehend
Sometimes God needs them in a greater plan
You bring your child into this world, there's nothing you
        wouldn't do
To hold her, love her and see her through.

A loving daughter, wife and mother
A loving sister, friend and lover
Loved by many in her short time here
Impressions left by the love she shared.

Life is short, never guaranteed
Love one another, help another in need
Take care of those you love as they care for you
Never take life for granted for one day it may be you.

Dedicated to Bobbi Sue Reynolds
In loving memory

I do not know the quiet night
It doesn't exist while I fight
I do not know peaceful rest
It doesn't allow me forgetfulness.

Existence runs far away from me
I only have a one-track mind
I secretly still stand on guard
Observant of my surroundings near and far.

Civilians know not a soldier's life
No idea we're still living to fight
Some say we're not the same once we're home
We relive our battlebuddies' lives who are gone.

We are soldiers, nothing is ever the same
We move forward when they call our names
Without hesitation we answer the call
All gave some, some gave all.

When our service is over it isn't done
We still will stand as an army of one
We won't back down or fall in the cracks
We are battlebuddies, we have each other's back.

SHE wasn't expecting to lose her legs
It all happened so fast
Her life changed forever instead
She didn't know what hit her... crash!

Overseas, the convoy was hit
Three died instantly, one survived
Embedded in his memory, wishing he could forget
That IED that took his battlebuddy's life.

They married young, he made her happy everyday
He was drafted when she found out she was with child
He never got to see their twins born in May
But the twins had his eyes and smile.

One thing is certain *It won't happen to me* you've always said
You can't change or go back and undo circumstance
Live life to the fullest, live with no regrets
Never quit, always go the distance.

I can't find my glasses, I thought I put them there
I can't remember the life I knew, the love I always shared
I can't form my words as good as I did before
Just keep reminding me who I am once more.

I know it may get frustrating, please be patient with me
I've gotten older and my mind is going away quickly
Know that I love you, in my heart I know who you are
Sometimes I may wander off a little too far.

Time will vanish so please keep on being strong
We never know what life will give us in our journey long
Don't you cry for you did your very best
Just keep our memories since I tend to forget.

Where is Freddie Don? He needs to come to bed
I can't sleep without him so I'll stay awake instead
I'm so tired now there's just no way to know
If I'll remember yesterday or if my mind will lose control.

I don't know what day it is or the year we're in
Have you seen my glasses or know where I put them?
I haven't been asleep in the chair, I only dozed off for a few
I don't have dementia, I know me better than you.

Dedicated to my mom

I hold you, you're not even here
You're in my heart, in my arms
I can't have you where you belong
With me.

I have these dreams of us
Laughing, gazing into each other's eyes
We've secretly wanted this, impossible
We want what we can't have.

There's always hope I can hold onto
I know it's not enough yet enough for me
Having a true friend, I couldn't ask for more
Be still... in my dreams.

Your beauty is captivating, taking my breath away
You are here with me, yet I can't touch you
I can't have you where you belong
As we love in my dreams.

YOU interfere inside all my thoughts
I can't escape the thought of you
It's torturing me, paralyzing
I can't hear your voice yet.

Nobody can know, *hush hush*
Keep it on the downlow
Nothing can come of this we tell each other
Circumstances get in the way.

Can you feel me touch you with my words?
If that's all we can do, is that enough?
Though I touch you without touching you
From miles away.

In my thoughts we're dancing on the floor
I hold you in frame, I lead you
I pull you in, my hands running up your hips
We tango.

Heartbeat grows faster, it's racing
Everything is a mystery, intoxicating
Reading between the lines, I read you
I can't put you down, I'm so intrigued.

I should've taken the time to hug you
Before I walked out the door
I should've paid attention while you were in my room
To tell you I love you more.

I should've held back my words I used
Instead of using my words like a knife
I didn't mean to hurt the best of me... you
I just wanted to be right.

I shouldn't have put off the things needed done
For I thought I had tomorrow instead of today
I have no idea if tomorrow will come
Or when the Good Lord will carry me away.

Never leave words left unspoken
Don't ever go to bed with regret
You never know where you're going
Sometimes it's easy to forget.

This is about being so consumed with day to day busyness,
we forget what is most important, the people we love,
the people we'll pass by.
Make a change and a difference to those who matter most
and those who long to matter

Nine years ago feels like yesterday
I held your hand as the angels carried you away
Prince of Peace written all across my mind
As I saw your body say *Goodbye.*

I'm not bitter because you left
Just missing your love and kisses on my head
Red birds surround me and I know it's you
Their voices sing *Char it'll be ok someday soon.*

Fall leaves drop to the ground, your favorite season here
It's been so long since I touched you, 9 long years
I still hear you saying *Don't cry for me*
Daddy, it's just hard and I feel so empty.

Haven't prepared your mansion & streets of gold
Here on earth was never day was never your home
As I live on each passing day through
When I see a red bird I'll know that it's you.

I'll give momma your love, so we can get that smile
You know she'll be there after awhile
Until then she'll feel your love in her thoughts
Just like she did the first day you won her heart.

WHEN our Savior takes you home
How can I really understand?
When losing you here will steal my every breath
For your earthly home will be no more.

Yes, I know, you won't suffer any longer
You'll be absent from any pain
Filled with joy and peace
You'll see your loved ones again.

When our Savior takes you home
We'll gather to say our farewell
Will you still come to me in my dreams or will I feel you near?
For I'll miss the times we goofed off & the times we held
        each other close.

I know someday I'll see you there
Though I know not when I'll come
I'll meet you and dad at heaven's gate
When the angels carry me home.

YOU'RE the only love story I want to read
The only heart that beats with mine
The only touch I want to feel
The only woman I want always with me.

Your hands are enough for me to hold
In winter, spring, summer or fall
I want to live life with you
Having you with me I couldn't fail.

I look into your eyes and I become lost
I don't want to be found
You are my peace , you are my calm
My voice when I can't speak but I have so much to say.

Do you know you're the freshest rose that I long to smell?
The lyrics in my song
The oxygen that gives me breath
The whisper of an angel.

SHE tore back my chest
Exposing my heart
Touched it with her hands
Promising to handle it with care.

She looked through my eyes
To get into my soul
Reading it through like a book
Fascinated by what it said.

She took my smile
Widening it by flexibility
She brushed over it with hers
Showing me I wasn't smiling before.

She etched the word *Love*
Her actions wrote inside
Just listen to her heart beating
It beats with yours.

YOU don't have to say you love me
Because your actions say you do
You don't have to say of me you dream
Because I'm dreaming of you too.

Love is built on a foundation strong
It is solid, firm, it will never break
Loving each other we could never go wrong
We have so much love to make.

I've thought of you way before you came
I knew one day you'd appear
I've searched life over until the day
I knew you'd come to me & now the day is here.

I've now learned the thing's I do not want
I've learned of lessons that helped me grow
I won't rush this love
I never want to lose our love so strong.

YOU can't make somebody love you
God knows I've tried
Later in years I realized it's my love I need
I'm reaching out for me, unavailable.

All I know is what bars I've put up
All I know is how to keep myself at bay
Love is dangerous, my heart bleeding
When is it safe to unlock these chains?

Set me free from the traps I've set
It's time that I live, that I love
I'm scared where will I roam?
After being locked up for life.

If I ask for help then I'm needy
If I love me then I'll be too clingy
If I draw in a certain crowd I like
They'll be my next mistake.

I've made up my mind
No more being tormented in my head
Nothing more I'll allow in my way
I'm gonna love me, I'm gonna fight this hell.

IT'S hard to believe that you're gone
You wouldn't have it no other way
You gave your life in the blazing sun
There are no words left to say.

I see all the pictures of the memories
I see you and the slideshow plays
I feel you everywhere, you're beside me
Since you gave your life and passed away.

You wouldn't trade heaven for earth down here
You died a happy man, loving what you done
You would tell me *Daulton, dry those tears*
Always remember Soldier on.

You don't come back the same
Half of you is left in that foreign land
Life doesn't stop but you remain
United we stand!

Dedicated to Sgt Ken Harris Jr

TRUCKS were rolling, mission ready
Pulling out of camp, something is wrong
Everything started steadily
Brakes slammed, he was gone.

He came home, served in many units, he was in mine
He couldn't take the pressure anymore
Marriage on the rocks, he ended his life
His battlebuddies didn't get to say goodbye.

Their battlebuddies felt the loss
We returned back to our homes
Something died in us when we counted the cost
We mourned the moment they were gone.

We visit their headstones, missing them even more
They wouldn't want us to cry
Tears stream down but they understand what for
As we honor these memories, he'd say no regrets
        when I died for the war.

In loving memory
Sgt Harris & Sgt Denham

JUST touch my body
As if you were trying to find your way on a map
Trace your route on me
Drive straight through on me.

I just need to feel you traveling around my curves
As you move through them slowly
Your fingers going around me cautiously
Then you brake enough to catch my breath.

There are no red lights in your way
No caution signs, just me
Waiting to be discovered on your back road
Where you feel free to roam.

Highlight the important parts of your trip
Highlight me upon your fingertips
I'll hold myself in place patiently
Bare in front of your skin.

LONG and spiraled hair
A sundress, t-shirts or a pair of jeans
Everyone fell for her looks
Nobody could touch her heart.

Who knew this young, beautiful girl?
Who thought they did?
You didn't know you couldn't have
She was deep inside her wall.

Countless times, femininity equals *unsafe*
Countless times her body, raped
An every-day smile put things to rest
Nobody able to guess.

That long and spiraled hair
She slowly cut off, piece by piece
Different lifestyle left everyone confused
She found her safe place & who she was always meant to be.

Where did she go? No sundress to wear
She traded them for men's pants instead
Oh the hell she took in stride
Gang-raped, once again, another part of her died.

Dedicated to my truth

HER feet make her stumble and fall
There's nothing that medicine will cure
Wrinkled hands that worked once before
Her body so fragile, a heart that's aching.

I hold her hand, I take her in my arm's
I kiss her forehead then I see her smile
The weight of her pain I put on me
She's the wind beneath my wings.

She's always been the strongest woman I've known
She feels embarrassed because she's lost her strength
I love her through it, mostly I feel it's not enough
Roles reversed, compared to her I'm not too tough.

She's loved by thousands all over
A heart that beats for each and every one
She has become legendary though she has no idea
I'm honored to call her *Mother!*

I sift through the chapters in my life
The times I failed, cried and smiled
The times when I took care of everyone but me
I've lived, I've loved and I've survived.

Every chapter I've learned who I am
What my purpose is on earth
Each time I've been knocked down
I always get back up, I rise again.

I have no need for recognition or sympathy
No silver or gold, no materialistic value
I crave with each breath I take to be loved, to belong & fit
I patiently hope that love will find me & I'll find the place
        that is safe.

I reach, I stretch for a hand to hold
Comfort I give to all in need
How does it feel to receive?
I want to taste, feel, to be something to someone.

SHE walks upon a log onto the water
Bending down, her fingers dance in the water
Nobody around to hear her cry, to listen
Nature will, the water embraces her loneliness.

Only the birds that sing are her music
She asks for the angels to embrace this life
They gently whisper into the wind
You're no longer alone, just look up.

Simplicity, quiet, free from harm
All she needs is for someone to love her
Many call, wave at her, maybe even laugh
Inside her soul it's bleeding only to stain.

Peace be still my lady, run away no more
All your fears have now deceased
You rise above to new beginnings
Now spread your wings, you must fly.

There is another soul listening
My arms reach out to catch you
Fall back into these arms
Come back to me, I won't let go.

Dedicated to my child within

LOVING WAY PART 2

I went back there today
I haven't seen this house in 31 year's
There's that reason I never wanted to stay
My eyes leaked many tears.

627 Loving Way stole my innocence
I was getting closure until I was there again
Just the reminder of hidden memories existing
Those bricks and clay closed me in.

Drove alongside the den
The driveway, that screened-in porch
I saw the scars hit me as hard as bricks
Wounds so deep, my memory scorched.

As I looked quickly time turned
It was time to bid farewell
I'm no longer here to serve
I became a survivor and I live to tell.

WITH YOU

I am myself, I do not falter my position
I am strong, I know not defeat
I survive life experiences
 I am the element of surprise.

I am the waves in the ocean, the sea to your shore
I am one with the night, I can be your sun
I hold my own in the center of a storm
I am the glue that holds you together.

I am the paper on which you write
The lyric you find in song
I never accept defeat, I will not waver
In the position in which I take.

Do not tell me what I wanna hear
In that way I can't adjust, I am I alone
I will not run away, I won't fall behind
Don't count me out before the end of life's fight.

STRANGLED

YOU'VE led a life we try to understand
As you utter *I'm sorry* in every other word
We've lived a life being beaten by your hand
Now the pain surfaces, our hearts... burned.

Sunday night, I felt your hate for your own blood
As you left me beaten and bruised
Determined to destroy what you knew you would
Not realizing all that you had to lose.

Now I am left strangled, I lie here, breathless
The rage I still see beneath you is still alive
I sleep, covered by your thoughtlessness
Dreaming of the night I almost died.

Strangled, beaten, bruised
Daughter, sister, caregiver of all
With nothing left to lose
I must go into the night alone.

TO TELL YOU THE TRUTH

I am not a case or situation
I am not a label you can frame
I am no longer a victim of frustration
Once a child who survived the rapes.

You no longer can control my strength
I no longer can hold my head down low
Now I'm able to lift my voice and speak
Of all the things I buried years ago.

All of my emotions are ready to be heard
The silence is now broken, I shall hide no more
Always dreamed of being like a bird
Flying to a place I now can soar.

TO TELL YOU THE TRUTH
YOU CAN KEEP LIVING IN YOUR DENIAL
KEEP TELLING YOURSELF YOU'VE DONE NOTHING WRONG
DAMN YOU TO THE HELL THAT WILL CAPTURE YOUR SPIRIT
FOR NOW GOD IS IN CONTROL.

AWAY FROM HOME

THE roll call was shouted intensely
You knew if your name was called
You were on the next mission
No discussion only time to move.

Dressed in full battle rattle
Fear was all that was known
Bridges blown up everywhere
The evidence of bullets were engraved
Displaying a gallery of them on the truck.

You couldn't recognize the stars or the moon
They were shadowed by the mortar attacks
The lasers, RPG's, blazing the clouds
The sounds you heard was the music we nodded off to.

Our bullet-proof vest was our blanket
MRE's were our food
Never knowing when we'd get full again
It always affected our mood.

AT&T calling card, best friend on our side
It always let us hear mom's voice
Telling us of letters sent our way
She sends her love each day.

Written in Iraq

MISSING YOU MY LOVE

YOU don't see my arms wrap around you
Or the tears I wipe off your face
You don't feel the way my head lays on the pillow beside you
Or the way I travel with you to each place.

You don't feel the way I run my fingers through your hair
Or the way I watch you brush your teeth
If you could only feel what you don't see
You could feel me.

You don't hear me speak your name in every other word
Or cry wishing you were near
You don't hear me whisper sweet nothings like I always did
If you could only hear.

I'd give anything to smell the scent off your body
Or smell the roses you once gave
I'd give anything to smell supper cooking in our kitchen
Or the smell of the home we once made.

You don't see me wrap my arms around you
You don't feel my fingers run through your hair
You don't hear me speak your name in every other word
And I'm not the same without you near.

Written in Kuwait

ACKNOWLEDGMENTS

*I would first love to acknowledge God! All my life I've known God,
thanks to my parents who raised me and my siblings in church.
God is why I am literally still breathing today. He honored his
word when I was in combat. I sustained combat injuries that were
meant to take my life, but he kept me breathing when I could've
easily taken my last breath. He brought me back home so I could
continue to take care of my parents. I'll never forget that. He has
never given up on me even when there was more than one occasion
that I had given up. I owe him everything.*

*I would love to acknowledge my parents. I give them thanks for
raising me up in church: the greatest thing they did for me though
as a kid growing up I didn't always want to attend. I also thank
them for giving back to children by becoming house parents, raising
foster children when their birth parents couldn't. I respect them so
much for that. It gave us an even bigger family to be a part of. Our
family was blessed.*

*I would like to acknowledge all of my battlebuddies I had the hon-
or of serving beside from Basic Training up through combat in Iraq.
Each of them changed and shaped my life, and we have always had
each other's six. I would take a bullet for all of them. They have the
best of me. I salute them all.*

123

ABOUT THE AUTHOR

I am Charlotte Daulton, a daughter, sister, aunt, caregiver, friend and an Army combat veteran. I turned 42 in September of 2017. I've led an interesting life, I should say.

I became an adult at six- years old. My innocence and childhood ended then because I was molested by a foster brother who my parents raised. He was older than me. I didn't have a childhood once the sexual abuse begin. I wasn't able to tell anyone or confide in my family because their reputation would have been threatened if I ever spoke of this.

In my teenage years I was raped by someone else. I was the baby in the family, but, please, believe me when I say I wasn't spoiled. My parents raised us in a strict fashion. We never had "the" talk. In our biological family there was a son and two daughters. My sister and I didn't even know what happened to a girl once puberty hit.

Every time the church doors opened, we were there. When I was born, my parents worked at an orphan home & school. They were house parents. Mom was also the school secretary. Among other things, she was known as The Tylenol Lady.

I often thank God that my parents worked there. The older kids took turns babysitting me until the home shut down. They showed me so much love and still do to this day. I love them like blood relatives.

My classmates made fun of and picked on me because I wasn't rich. We were poor, and I'm grateful because it taught me that material things are insignificant. I would rather be rich in love and have the little things be the big things.

In 1994 I began working in a nursing home where I found my calling in the healthcare field. I learned so much about compassion and loving others, and it humbled me. Each time a patient died, it literally broke my heart. I worked as a CNA from 1994-2005. In 1996 I enlisted in the Army. I originally signed the line with my best friend at the time so that she wouldn't have to be alone in that difficult time. The day came to board the plane to Basic Training, and she didn't show.

I had never been away from home. I was scared, and at the reception station I tried to get out of going. But I had a change of heart. I'm so glad. My reason for serving my country changed. I wanted to learn my own strengths and weaknesses, I wanted order and discipline for my life. I wanted to be somebody, and this was my shot.

I did it for my battlebuddies once training began. I knew I was supposed to stay the course with them. This was the defining moment of my life.

At this point I had to keep my sexuality to myself because back in 1997 it was a don't-ask-don't-tell policy. I wasn't about to jeopardize my situation. I didn't hit on anybody (that was the furthest from my mind). I was on a mission, so I kept everything hush hush.

I was in the Army Reserves which is how I had separate careers: one as a civilian working in the nursing home and another as an 88mike (better known as truck driver).

In 2003 I got the call to deploy for Operation Enduring & Iraqi Freedom. I got put in a unit that needed soldiers in order to ship *out overseas. I'll never forget having to write my will while I was in my 20's: what a sobering experience. When mom dropped me off in Memphis, that definitely was the hardest goodbye I ever said. I cried for a moment then collected myself. We boarded the Greyhound bus, strangers waving us off.*

At Ft Campbell, we got all our vaccinations and legal papers written and signed. We also got our new uniforms. I'll never forget being at the airport hanger: I called everybody and told them what they meant to me because there was that 50/50 chance that I would not come back or that I might return in a bodybag.

I sustained 5 serious combat injuries. I have a traumatic brain injury (TBI) where I suffered 50% bone loss, chronic Ptsd, chronic pain. I am also a military sexual trauma survivor. I was gang-raped by my own 2 Sergeants. I took them through a court martial, and that's as far as I'm going to discuss that rape.

I loved my job in the Army. My battlebuddies gave me new meaning to life. Except for those 2 Sergeants, the rest of my unit was awesome. We keep in touch often. Altogether since the war, I've lost 5 battlebuddies who paid the ultimate sacrifice. I miss them like crazy. When you have a battlebuddy die in the field, you face hell itself. You cry. You have night terrors. Those days play like a slideshow you're watching everyday.

I got medevaced home on June 7, 2004. They gave me no say in the matter, and I still hate myself for being shipped back home even though the reason wasn't my fault. I was medically retired on October 15, 2004.

I was a caregiver to both my disabled parent's before and after the war. We lost my dad at age 67: nine years ago. I was holding his hand when he took his last breath. That killed me inside. I had to make the arrangements with my mom: the floral arrangements, the slideshow for people to watch, and the music for the visitation and funeral. I went ahead then and purchased a double headstone. I'm still caring for mom who has stage 7 dementia and stage 4 Parkinsons. She is my beautiful, my everything. We're best friends. Those are the cruelest diseases. I have been on an emotional rollercoaster because of it. We almost lost my mom recently, but she's a fighter.

As I referenced earlier, I am also a lesbian. I respect my family and everyone who I come across. I am me, and I am going to live my life without regrets. I have a lot of lifestyle-related poetry, moments when I knew love and the struggle. I endured a lot of hateful people when I first came out. I swear every straight woman thinks they are going to be hit on. It's not the case with me. I respect others and I expect the same basic respect back. I lost a lot of friends when I came out. Looking back, it was definitely their loss, not mine. They weren't friends to begin with.

I still believe in God. I do study the Bible. I can't go to a church that proclaims to love me yet every time they see me at church I always interrogate me regarding my lifestyle. I go to worship God. I don't care what other's think about me in that regard. It's not about them. We are all supposed to only worship him when we come to church. I am still a Christian. I love how everyone from my family, friends and battlebuddies, co-workers love me for who I am as Charlotte not just the lesbian named Charlotte.

My poetry collection is based on my life experiences. These are pieces of me that I want to share. If I can survive everything I have written about, then not only can I survive anything... so can you! I hope as you read through these pages that you will find that you can relate to at least one of my poems. I hope that it gives you strength and power to get through your difficult or challenging situation.

God bless, Ya'll, and I hope that you enjoyed this book.

PHOTO GALLERY

PIECES OF ME

Dad and me at my graduation from basic training
Ft Leonard Wood, MO

My 1st Sgt and me in Kuwait on my first mission

Perkins and me at the Ft Campbell barracks

Perkins and me at the welcome home ceremony in Millington TN

Torkell and me boarding the plane at Ft Campbell

1st platoon in Taji, Iraq

The trucks of the 212th Transportation

Waiting to get the call to unload our fuel in Baghdad

KJ and me in Taji, Iraq

The Truckville sign

Me at Sgt Harris' grave

At Sgt Harris' grave with his battlebuddies and family

Dad's grave

Mom and me

Mom and me

Mom and me

Mom and me at prom in assisted living

My shadow box

Me at Myrtle Beach SC

.

CPSIA information can be obtained
at www.ICGtesting.com
Printed in the USA
BVHW01s2230271217
50369 1BV00001B/59/P